. Written by Surinder Singh
Edited by Pamela Weaver
Photographed by Surinder Singh

C000098773

Printed on 14th Feb 20012
 Distributed in United States of America by
Amazon.com

 ISBN 13 978-1467908276

Printed in Charleston, SC. USA

Introduction

The purpose of this book is as suggested by the title-
Rasoyee. Rasoyee means in Indian a home kitchen.
Most of the curries can be cooked in ordinary kitchen
and will taste same as they taste in many well known
restaurants. I will start by explaining a very small
but essential range of spices and fresh herbs which
can be stored in your kitchen. We will make some
starters and dips, different types of onions dishes with
some basic but popular curries, few different types of
rice too. There's even a thorough explanation on how to
make chapattis! In almost every Indian curry dish
we use a mixture called _Turka_ and I will simplify
the way to make _Turka. After reading this you will be_
able to cook delicious Indian starters, tasty curries
and the must have sides of rice and chapattis.

Contents

Chilli Powder

Paprika

Turmeric Powder

Garam masala

Curry Powder

Larder

To start any kind of cooking, we need some kind of basic ingredients in the larder. Some of the basic ingredients used in an Indian kitchen.

Salt: - We all know what salt is, we do not need to explain it.

Chilli Powder: - Powder made from dried red hot chillies.

Paprika: - Paprika is a spice made from grinding of dry fruits of Capsicum, bell peppers or hot chilli peppers. It has a caramel smoky taste and dominant red colour in curry.

Turmeric Powder: - Turmeric Powder, called Haldi in Indian is a woody aroma; yellow coloured spice is rhizomatous, herbaceous perennial plant of ginger family.

Curry Powder: - Curry powder is an aromatic blend of some Indian spices and gives good flavour to food.

Garam-masala: - Garam-masala is from Hindi (hot) and masala (mixture) is a basic blend of ground spices common in India.

Black Lychee   Jeera Whole   Methi

Cloves

Bay Leafs   Cinnamon St   Dhania whole

Jeera Powder: Jeera, commonly known as cumin seed. Name cumin drawn from old French has a strong, warm and distinct flavour. This aromatic seed is very common in Indian curries, but it also can be used in Mexican, and old Roman dishes.

Dhania; - Dhania is a coriander seeds. It is used as a thickener in curries and is nutty and orangey flavoured.

Black Lychee: - It is a common ingredient in Indian Cooking. Cardamom has a unique intensely astringent aromatic fragrance not bitter, but coolness.

Methi: - Methi is a fenugreek leaves. They are medium square leaves are of bitter taste and used in almost every curry.

Bay leafs: - This aromatic leaf, dried or fresh can be used in cooking for its distinct flavour and fragrance. Bay leafs are often used in Indian dishes specially Biryanies and different rice's.

Cloves: - Cloves are aromatic dried flower buds grown in Asia and in India under the name of Laung. Cloves are used in most of Indian cuisine, mainly in pilao rice and biryanies. Also used in aromatic tea and medicinal purpose to heat the body.

Cinnamon stick:- Cinnamon sticks come from bark trees with a strong aromatic flavour. It is very commonly used condiment in most of the curries (meat), and rice and every kind of sweets Asian or European

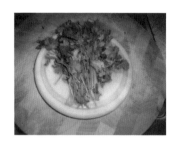 

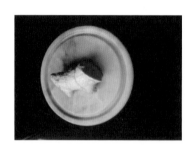 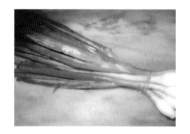

Fresh Herbs

Ginger: Ginger is one of the main ingredients in Indian cooking. Fresh finely chopped ginger is used to make curry for flavor and short time preservation,

Garlic: Garlic is as raw and finely chopped is used in almost all the curry dishes as condiment, seasoning and for flavor.

Green Chilies: Chilies are used in curry just for strength and flavor of the curry. They are strong and hot by taste. They give a tangy flavor.

Coriander: - Fresh coriander or coriander leafs are used to garnish and flavor the curry in Asian cooking. You just sprinkle finely chopped coriander, before serving the dish.

Spring onion: Spring onions are also used in curries purely for flavor and for bit of a colour.

Green peppers: Green pepper is a highly prized condiment with hot and pungent taste, used in curries for flavor.

Turka

Half a inch of Ginger (Root)
Three medium size Onion
Four cloves Garlic
Couple of Chilies
Two table spoon Methi leafs
Two medium Tomato
50ml of Cooking Oil or Ghee

Turka, yes Turka is the basic of all Indian Curries. Most of the curries you make, you need Turka. And the ammount of Turka depends on the ammount of curry you are making. Generaly speaking, we take a ammount to be for two people.

To make a Turka for two, take a deep pan . Add 50ml of cooking oil or ghee, add finly chopped ginger, garlic, some chilies to your taste into a pan. Put the Pan on a gas mark four. Put two table spoon of methi. And cook it for ten or fifteen minutes till the onions go soft and brown. You can put two or three chopped tomatos, stir till everything go nice and soft. Now add quarter pint of hot water, and let it simmer for five minutes. This fine past is called Turka.

You can use this little beauty for any medium curry.

Curry Sauce

Curry sauce in Indian cooking is regarded as a base for almost all curries. We can make curries of different strength and taste by just adding different ingredients to this medium curry sauce.

Two onions
Half inch of ginger
Four cloves garlic
Two tomatoes
Fresh coriander
50ml of cooking oil or Ghee

To make curry sauce, we need to make Turka. Dice the two onions into a deep pan. Add finely chopped ginger and garlic, two tomatoes into the same pan.
Next add 50ml of cooking oil. Put the pan on gas mark three and cook it till onions go brownish.
Now add tea spoon of salt, half of chili, one of turmeric powder, one of curry powder one of tomato puree. Let it simmer for five minutes, occasionally stirring the mixture. Now add three quarter of a pint of hot water. Simmer again for ten minutes, and then liquidize it to a fine paste.
Garnish with finely chopped coriander.
That's your medium curry sauce ready to serve.

Patia Curry Sauce
Patia is sweet and Saur curry. To prepare we heat the amount of curry sauce we need (as we explained above) to the boiling point and add two spoons of Patia sauce, let it boil of another five minutes .
Patia curry sauce is ready to serve. Add a piece of sliced lemon or tomato to look nice.

Korma Sauce

Korma is a very mild sauce. To make korma sauce we put the amount of sauce into the pot an start heating on gas mark three .Whilst heating curry sauce add some coconut cream. Normally a spoon per person is enough. Once the coconut cream dissolves add some single cream (to your taste) and bring it to the boil. Your Korma sauce ready to serve. Add a piece of tomato and a leaf of coriander to garnish.

Masala Sauce

There are two types of masala sauces usually used. One is masala sauce which we make now and makhni masala sauce which will be explained further on.

Put the amount of curry sauce you need into the pot and put on a gas mark three to boil. Once start boiling add very fine chopped green peppers and onions. Also add a serving spoon of grinded cashew nuts, powdered almonds and some single cream as per your taste. Simmer it for at least for ten minutes before serving.

Before serving garnish the dish with some cashews and pistachios sprinkled on top. You may put some almond flakes on top as well for decoration.

Patia Sauce

100grams Tomato Ketchup
20ml Lemon Juice
500 grams Mango Chutney

Take a slightly deep container, and put say 100 grams of tomato ketchup and 500 grams of mango chutney add 20 ml litters of lemon juice. All you need to do now is liquidize the mixture to fine runny past.
That is your Patia sauce.

Salsa Curry Sauce

To make salsa curry sauce, put some already made medium curry sauce you think you need into a pan and put on gas mark three till it comes to the boil. When it comes to boil add already made salsa sauce according to your taste to it and let it simmer for ten minutes. Add fresh coriander to it. Salsa sauce is ready to serve, add some garnish like a piece of tomato and coriander leaf to look nice.

Chili Curry Sauce

Same as other curry sauces, we put the amount of already made medium curry sauce into a pan and bring it to the boil on gas mark three. When it comes to boil add pre-prepared chili sauce into it, amount depending on your taste. Let it simmer for ten minutes before serving.

Serve it with little bit of coriander on top, a piece of tomato and some very fine chopped chilies on top.

Makhni Masala Sauce

Makhni Masala is a mild sauce with very rich taste. To make Makhni Masala, put the amount of medium curry sauce you need into the pot to boil on gas mark three. Once it starts boiling add Rogan Josh sauce, according to your taste (say one table spoon per portion) with some single cream. Bring it to boil and then let it simmer for ten minutes.

Before serving garnish the dish with some cashews and pistachios sprinkled on top. Put some almond flakes on top as well for decoration.

Rogan Josh Sauce

5 Table spoon of Ghee
Small tin of plum tomato
1 litter single cream
50 grams of whole zeera
50 grams of whole Dhania
2 table spoons of Methi

Take a deep pan and put 5 spoonful of ghee and heat it on Gas marks two for two minutes. Now add 50 grams of zeera, 50 grams of Dhania powder, and 2 table spoons of Methi and heat it for two minutes. Next add one tin of plum tomatoes and a liter of single cream, let it simmer for half an hour.

Now add 200grams of cashew nuts into that mixture, half a spoon of red cooking color and grind the mixture till it's really smooth and pasty. Let it cool to settle of an hour or so.
Rogan josh sauce is ready to use in any curry.

Salsa Sauce

Tree medium Onions
Three Peppers (Red, Green and yellow each)
Sugar (3table spoons)

Chop three medium size onions, dice them and put them in a medium pot with just quarter liter of water. Let it simmer for ten minutes. Now dice the peppers into quarter inch thickness. By this time onions will be soft, put those sliced papers in with the onions add half tea spoon of salt, same of chilies powder, and of zeera, Dhania, garam masala with 60 ml of malt vinegar and black papers. Now put 100 to 150 ml litters of tomato ketchup. Add three table spoon of sugar. Let it simmer another ten minutes and that's your salsa sauce ready to cool down.

Chili Sauce
100 grams Fresh Chilies
100 ml Cooking Oil
Tin of plum tomatoes

Put some chilies in the pot with 100 ml of oil, tin of plum tomatoes and put on gas mark four. Boil it for fifteen minutes at least. Now add a spoon full of salt, chilies powder, zeera, Dhania, paprika. Let it simmer for ten more minutes. Now liquidize to a nice and smooth sauce. That is your chilies sauce.

Patia Sauce
100grams Tomato Ketchup
20ml Lemon Juice
500 grams Mango Chutney

Take a slightly deep container, and put say 100 grams of tomato ketchup and 500 grams of mango chutney add 20 ml litters of lemon juice. All you need to do now is liquidize the mixture to fine runny past. That is your Patia sauce.

Starter Sauces and Dips

Pink Sauce

500 grams of natural yogurt
Half spoon of Mint puree
150 ml of tomato-ketchup
Pinch of Red food colour

Pink sauce is the most popular of the starter sauces. Take 500 grams of natural yogurt in a deep container or mixing bowl. Add half a table spoon of salt, half of chili powder, half of Garam-masala, half of mint puree and five or 150 ml of tomato-ketchup with a little pinch of red colour. Mix it gently to a smooth sauce.
That is a Pink Sauce.

Red Sauce

Two large Onions
Two medium tomatoes
Fresh coriander
Two spoons of lemon juice

To make the well known red sauce that is served in restaurants start by chopping two large onions in a deep container add two medium tomatoes, fresh coriander. Add some water (depends how thick you like your sauce) and liquidize it. Now add table spoon of salt, chili-powder, Garam-masala, freshly chopped coriander and two spoons of lemon juice with a pinch of red colour. Mix and liquidize to a smooth sauce.
That is a Red Sauce.

Mint Sauce

500 grams of Yogurt
2 table spoons of Mint puree

Mint sauce is a white yogurt sauce. To make it, again put 500 grams of yogurt in a deep container. Then add the spices, half table spoon of salt, half of chili, half of Garam-masala, then add two of mint- puree. Mix them all well.
Sprinkle little fresh coriander over it and Mint Sauce is ready to serve.

Tamarind Sauce

Tamarind is a sweet and Saur flavored seeded pod. To make it into a sauce, we need to soak Tamarind into three times the amount of it into water for few hours preferably overnight.

After that put the mixture into deep bowl and mix hard and briskly so that the water is mixed with tamarind and the seed are separated.

Now drain it back in the bowl. Chop two large onions, two tomatoes, some fresh coriander. Then put spoon of salt, half to one spoon of chili powder (according to your taste), half of Garam-masala, one of sugar, some lemon juice and five spoon of tomato-ketchup. Liquidize the lot into a smooth paste. You could dilute it according to your taste.

With a sprinkle of fine chopped coriander Tamarind Sauce is ready.

Spiced Onions

Three large Onions
Two table spoon of Mango-chutney
One table spoon of Mint-puree
Four table spoon of Tomato-ketchup
Some fine chopped coriander

Spice onions are very easy to make. Just dice two large onions into quarter centimeter cubes. Put them into a mixing bowl. Add tea spoon of salt half of chili powder, half of Garam-masala, two table spoon of mango-chutney, one table spoon of mint puree, four table spoon of tomato ketchup and tea spoon. Now all you have to do is mix it well and thoroughly. Spices can be changed according to personal taste. Sprinkle very fine chopped coriander on top and Spiced Onions are ready.

Onion Salad

Two medium size red onions
Two medium size tomatoes
One third of a cucumber
Two shoots of spring onions
Two table spoons of lemon juice

Onion Salad is also known as special onions. To make onion salad, chop two medium size tomato, two medium size red onions, one third of a cucumber, two shoots of spring onions (make sure they are approximately one cm or less) and place them in a mixing bowl. Add half a tea spoon of salt, quarter of chili powder, quarter of Garam-masala, two table spoon of lemon juice. Mix them thoroughly. That is your Onion Salad ready for two people.

Pakoras

Four medium size Onions
Two medium size Potatoes
Small Cauliflower
One inch of Ginger
Five cloves of Garlic
Fifteen ml Lime juice
Mint puree
Gram flour

Dice up onions, potatoes, cauliflower as fine as you can. Put them into a mixing bowl. Grind two or three cloves of garlic with a piece of ginger add to the bowl. Next add two tea spoons of salt, one of chili powder, one of gram masala 30 ml of lime juice, spoon of mint puree. Mix them well and leave it for half hour

Add half kg of gram flour and some water into the bowl and mix it till the dough sticks together. Make bite size pieces and deep fry them at 170 degree centigrade till they go brown.

Serve them with fresh salad, red sliced onion and sauce of your choice.

Chicken Pakoras

250 grams of Gram flour
Two table spoon of Mint puree
20 ml Lemon juice
Three quarter pan of Cooking Oil
4 Chicken Breasts

Take a mixing bowl, put sliced chicken in it. Sprinkle one tea spoon of salt, ½ of chili powder, 1 table spoon of Tandoori past or masala, 20 ml of lemon juice. Mix them well and let them marinate for an hour or so.

Now in another bowl put quarter kg or 250 grams of gram flour, one table spoon of salt, one tea spoon of chili, crushed garlic and ginger, some green challis one table spoon of mint and add some water and beat them into smooth running mixture.

Now add the marinated chicken into the mixture and again mix them well. Leave it for a while, so that mixture sticks well to the chicken.

Heat the chip-pan to 170 degree or gas mark 5 on the cooker, similar heat as for cooking the chips. Now pick up a piece of chicken from the mixture, shake it against the walls of the bowl and dip in the oil to fry for 2-3 minutes till they are nice and crispy
Put on Greece proof paper. They are ready to serve with any sauce or dips with sliced raw onions.

Shami Kebabs

One pound Mince
One medium size Onion
Fresh Coriander
One spoon of mint puree
An inch of ginger
Five cloves of garlic

To make Shami Kebabs, put the mince into a mixing bowl. Grind half an inch of ginger and five cloves of garlic into the bowl Add a tea spoon of salt, half of chilli powder, half of garam-masala and half of curry - powder to the paste. Now finely chop fresh coriander, few leaf of mint and a spoon of methi and one spoon of Tandoori paste or powder add to the mince as well. Mix everything in the mixing bowl, very thoroughly. Roll them into two inch radius balls and press into about half inch thick circles keeping the round shape.

Heat pancake pan on a gas cooker on gas mark four for a minute. Spread little cooking oil on to the pan. Put these previously made kebabs on the pan. Cook them in that pan turning on to both sides from time to time till they turn dark brown.

Shami Kebabs are ready to serve with little salad, sliced red onions and some kind of sauce of your choice.

Vegetable Curry

2 Medium size Onions
Six clove garlic
One inch of ginger
6 medium potatoes
Half kg green peas
100 ml oil or 100 ml Ghee
Two table spoon of tomato puree
100 grams of plum tomatoes

Chopped the onions as fine as you can and put them into the pot with 100 ml of oil (Vegetable or cooking) or 100 ml of Ghee with fine chopped ginger, and garlic and put on gas mark 4. Now add table spoon of zeera, table spoon of Methi and fry till onion turn brown. Now add tea spoon of salt, half spoon of chili powder, spoon of turmeric powder, half spoon of paprika, spoon of tomato puree, 100 grams fresh tomatoes. Turn down the gas to mark 3 and let them simmer for five minutes, and keep stirring from time to time.

Now add peeled and chopped potatoes (about 1 inch square) and green peas stir them well and fry them for another five minutes. Add ¾ litter of boiling water, let it simmer till potatoes are easily breakable by spoon. (Usually around 20 minutes). Sprinkle fresh chopped coriander and some gram masala for flavor.

That is your vegetable curry ready to serve with rice and chapattis or Nan.

Dall Curry

Two Onions (Medium Size)
Four cloves of Garlic
Half inch of Ginger
100 grams of Red Lentils
80 ml of cooking oil or Ghee

Dall is an Indian name for Lentils. Dall curry is a very common and basic curry in India. It is very easy to digest and full of protein and goodness.

Now for cooking, take deep pan add100 grams of Red Lentils. Wash them thoroughly, drain them, and add a pint of cold water. Also add tea spoon of salt, half a spoon of chili powder and one spoon of turmeric powder. Put the pot on gas mark four and bring it to boil. Let it boil for ten minutes.

Now take a frying pan put 80 ml of cooking oil, put on gas mark four and let it heat. Add finely chopped two onions, ginger and garlic. Keep on frying till they become soft and brown.

By this time lentils are already cooked for ten minutes, and turned yellow and soft. Empty the content of frying pan into the pot, mix it well. Let it cook for five more minutes. Now sprinkle some garam masala and finely chopped coriander. Dall is ready to serve two people

34

Chicken Curry

100 gm. plum tomatoes
120 ml cooking oil
3 onions (Large)
Six clove garlic
Breast of Chicken (4 breasts deiced)
Fresh coriander
Two table spoon of tomato puree

Dice the three large onions as fine as you can, also chop half a bulb or six clove of garlic, quarter inch of ginger, put them into a pan with 120 ml of cooking oil. Put on a gas mark 4 add a table spoon of Methi and jeera. Fry them for five minutes till onions starts turning brown.

Add one tea spoon of salt, half of chili powder of turmeric powder, one of curry powder, spoon of tomato puree, and 100 grams of plum tomato, now stir it well and let it simmer for 10 minutes, occasionally stirring the mixture.

Now add the diced chicken to the past, stir it and turn the gas down to mark 3. Let it simmer for 10 minutes, occasionally stirring. Now add quarter liter of hot water. Let it simmer another 10 minutes then add freshly chopped coriander.

Chicken curry is ready to serve with rice, Nan or chapatti.

Chicken Curry Mild

100 gm. plum tomatoes
120 ml cooking oil
3 onions (Large)
Half clove garlic
Breast of Chicken (4 breasts deiced)
Fresh coriander
Two table spoon of tomato puree
100 ml of single cream

Dice the three large onion as fine as you can, also chop half bulb of garlic, quarter inch ginger, put them into a pan with 120 ml of cooking oil. Put the pan on a gas mark four and fry them for five minutes till onions starts turning brown.

Add one tea spoon of salt, half of chili powder of turmeric powder, one of curry powder, spoon of tomato puree, and 100 grams of plum tomato, now stir it well and let it simmer for next 10 minutes, occasionally stirring them.

Now add the diced chicken to the past, stir it and turn the gas down to mark 3. Let it simmer for 10 minutes, occasionally stirring. Now add quarter liter of hot water. Add fresh 100 ml of fresh single cream to the pan and let it simmer another ten minutes. Note that amount of cream depends on your own taste and how mild curry you prefer. It applies to any curry, lamb, beef, vegetable etc.

Chicken curry is ready to serve with rice, Nan or chapatti.

Chicken Curry Hot

100 gm. plum tomatoes
120 ml cooking oil
3 onions (Large)
Half clove garlic
Breast of Chicken (4 breasts deiced)
Fresh coriander
Two table spoon of tomato puree
Three or Four Green Chilies

Dice the three large onions as fine as you can, also chop half a bulb of garlic and half inch of ginger, put them into a pan with 120 ml of cooking oil. Put on a gas mark four, add a table spoon of Methi and jeera, add some fine chopped green chilies and fry them for five minutes till onions starts turning brown.

Add one tea spoon of salt, half of chili powder of turmeric powder, one of curry powder, spoon of tomato puree, and 100 grams of plum tomato, now stir it well and let it simmer for next 10 minutes, occasionally stirring them.

Now add the diced chicken to the past, stir it and turn the gas down to mark 3. Let it simmer for 10 minutes, occasionally stirring. Now add quarter liter of hot water. Let it simmer another 10 minutes then add freshly chopped coriander.

Chicken curry is ready to serve with rice, Nan or chapatti.
You can make any curry hot, Madras or extra hot by adding green chilies or chilies powder to it according to your taste.

Lamb curry

Three medium size Onions
100 grams Plum tomatoes
Six clove of garlic
One inch of ginger
120 ml oil or ghee
Fresh coriander (Finely chopped)
Half kg diced lamb

Dice couples of onion fine as you can, chop ginger and garlic. Put it in a pan with oil (cooking or vegetable or if precise ghee is more preferred) also add two table spoon of Methi, one of jeera whole, three black cardimums two inches of cinnamon stick and put it on gas mark 3. Cook it for about few minutes until onions are soft. We call this process as cooking *turka*.

Now since turka is ready we can put one tea spoon of salt, some chili powder (can add some freshly chopped chili if you like), curry powder, some paprika, spoon of turmeric powder add some tomato puree and fresh or plum tomatoes. Stir and cook for a minute and now add the diced lamb, mix them well. Cover with lid .Cook for about 20 to 25 minutes till you can see the oil oozing out of curry mix. Now add half a pint hot water, stir and cook for another 15 minutes. Sprinkle freshly chopped coriander and some garam masala.

That is your lamb curry ready to serve with rice and chapatti parantha or Nan.

Chicken Salsa

Four Chicken Breasts
Two Large Onions
One inch of Ginger
Six clove of Garlic
Two Peppers (Red and Green)
Fresh Coriander (Finely chopped)
Two table spoon of Sugar
Five ounce of vinegar
Black pepper
50 grams of tomato ketchup
Tin of plum tomatoes

Dice up the onions as fine as you can with nice finely chopped ginger and garlic in a pot. Add two table spoons of Methi, one spoon of Jeera whole add some cooking oil. Heat up at gas mark four till the onions go brown. Now add one tea spoon of salt, half of chili powder, turmeric powder, and curry powder. Stir them well. Now add tomato puree, some fresh or tined plum tomatoes and mix them well. Let it cook for ten minutes. Cut your chickens into small pieces and put into the pot. Now chop both peppers into small dices and again put into the pot. Cook them till chickens turn little brownish white.

It's time to add 2 table spoon of sugar, vinegar, about 50 grams of tomato ketchup, some black peppers, mix them well and cook for another five minutes. Now add one third of a pint of water and let it simmer for five minutes.

Now add freshly chopped coriander and some garam masala. That's your salad ready to serve with anything you like, rice, chapattis, Nan, tequila

Chicken Chili

Two Large onions
One inch of ginger
Six clove of garlic
Fifty grams Green chilies
Tin of plum tomatoes
Two Chicken Breasts
Fresh coriander (finely chopped)
80 ml cooking oil or Ghee

Finely chop your onions and put into a pot. Add chopped ginger and garlic into the same pot, add 80 ml cooking oil into it and let it cook for few minutes on gas mark tree till onions go little brown.

Now while this is going on we make a chilies sauce. In a separate pot put a tin of plum tomatoes, green chilies and cooking oil and cook it for fifteen minutes. Add half spoon of salt, chilies powder, grinded zeera and Dhania. Few minutes later liquidize them and chilies sauce is ready.

Now back to first pot, that turka is ready, add tea spoon of salt, chilies powder, turmeric powder some curry powder and tomato puree mix them well. Add two table spoons of Methi one of Jeera whole and let it cook for five minutes. Add chopped chickens, cook till they are light brownish in colour. It's time now to add chili sauce we made earlier, mix well and allow it simmer for ten minute.

Add freshly chopped coriander and sprinkle some gram masala on top, chili chicken ready to serve with rice, chapatti and Nan

Chicken Bhoona

Four chicken breasts
Three large onions
One inch of ginger
Six clove of garlic
Hand full of fresh coriander
Dried and powdered zeera, Dhania
150grms of plum tomatoes
80 ml of cooking oil Ghee

Bhoona is often thought of as hot curry. No, Bhoona is a spicy curry. And again to clear a difference, Karahi and Balties are different, they are Bhoona but with different strength and different taste and different spices.

Now to make Bhoona, dice the onions and put them into a deep pan with finely chopped ginger, garlic and 80 ml of cooking oil, also add two table spoons of Methi, one of Jeera whole. Heat on gas fire mark four till the onions turn brown and remember to stir occasionally. Once turka turn brown add spices. Add one tea spoon of salt, half of chilly, one of turmeric powder, one of curry powder, half of zeera, half of Dhania powder, spoon of tomato purry, and 150 grams of plum tomatoes. Turn the gas down to three and let it simmer for five minutes.

Chop the chicken breast into sizes of your liking. Now add chickens to the pot, stir and leave it to cook for about fifteen minutes occasionally stirring. Once the chicken is cooked (you can see the oil coming to top of curry or you can cut chicken with spoon) add a little water (about 25ml) to the curry and let it simmer for another five minutes.

Now add finely chopped fresh coriander and sprinkle few pinches of garam masala for a nice flavor. Bhoona is ready to serve with rice, Nan or chapatti.

Chicken Karahies

Two medium size onions
One inch ginger
Six clove of garlic
Tree medium size tomatoes
Half a dozen fresh spring onions
Two green peppers
Finely chopped Fresh coriander
80 ml cooking oil or Ghee

Karahi is medium curry, spicy but rich in flavored, not hot dish as some may think. To make Karahi, we make turka as usual. We chop onions into small dices, and put into a deep pan along with fine chopped ginger and garlic with two table spoons of Methi. Add 80 ml cooking oil into the pan and put on gas mark four to let it cook for ten minutes till onions go brownish. Now chop spring onions into small pieces, add to the pot, along with diced (quarter of an inch) green peppers, and stir well.

Now chop tomatoes into very small pieces and add into the pot. Add tea spoon of salt, half of chili powder, one of curry powder, half of turmeric powder, half of zeera and Dhania powder. Leave it to cook for few minutes then add little bit of water, mix them and let it cook another five minutes, before you add diced chickens into the pot. Let it simmer for at least fifteen minutes occasionally stirring. Try to cut the chicken with spoon and if you can then chicken is cooked

Finely sprinkle fine chopped fresh coriander and garam masala. That is chicken Karahi ready to serve with rice Nan or Chapatti

Chicken Balties

Four Breast of chickens
Three large onions
Six Shoots of spring onions
Two Green Peppers
Two or Three Green Chilies
Two Tomatoes (medium to large)
Hand full of fresh coriander finely chopped
80 ml cooking oil or Ghee

Balties are Hot and spicy flavored dish. To cook chicken Balti we have to make a spicy turka. To do that dice two onions and chop spring onions into small dices and put them into deep pan with 50ml of cooking oil or Ghee (whatever you prefer), and place on gas mark four. At this point add two table spoons of Methi, one of Jeera whole. Let it cook for ten minutes, stirring occasionally.

By this time the onions should be brownish and time to add spices. Chop green chilies and put into the pot. Add spoon of salt, half of chili powder, one of turmeric powder, one of curry powder, half of zeera, half of Dhania powder, half of paprika, couple of pinches of Methi. Mix them and leave on heat for five minutes. Put a spoon full of tomato puree and two chopped tomatoes into the mixture. Add 10ml of water and mix well, so that it becomes a smooth paste. Let it simmer for five minutes.

Now chop another onion and two green peppers slightly bigger than earlier and add to the pot. While that is cooking, dice the chickens into small pieces, add to pot cook it for fifteen minutes. Do not forget to stir from time to time. After that cut fresh coriander, sprinkle garam masala and coriander over the curry that's your chicken Balti ready to serve with rice, Nan, Chapatti.

Chicken Lalparies

Two large onions
Inch of ginger
Six cloves of garlic
Two green peppers
Fresh coriander
Half tin of plum tomato
  Or
Two fresh tomatoes
Four chicken breasts
100ml of house red wine
80 ml of cooking oil or Ghee

Lalparies are medium but spicy dish cooked in red wine. To start like most Indian curries we make turka. Dice onions, along with ginger and garlic into a pot with 80 ml of cooking oil or ghee and on gas mark four to heat. Add two spoons of Methi one of Jeera whole. Cook for four minutes till onions go brown. While onions are getting cooked, chop both pepper (red and green) into two to three inch long and quarter inch wide sticks, and dice the tomatoes.

Now as onions are browning add spices. Add one spoon of salt, half spoon of chilies, half of turmeric powder, half of curry powder, one table spoon of tomato puree, mix them and add chopped pepper and tomatoes, let it simmer for five minutes.

Cut chicken into inch or inch and half slices and add to the pot, cook until chicken is almost ready, then add 100ml of house red wine. Cook it for fifteen minutes. If the curry looks a little too dry then add little water.

Sprinkle fresh chopped coriander and garam masala. Now chicken Lalpari is ready to serve with rice, Nan, Chapattis.

Chicken Sharabi

Four Chicken Breasts
Two Medium size onions
Half inch of ginger
Half a clove of garlic
One red pepper
Six shoots of spring onion
Two med. size tomato
Fresh coriander
15 to 20 ml of Brandy
80 ml of cooking oil or Ghee

Chicken sharabi is a hot and spicy flavoured dish. As usual we start by making a turka. Peel and dice the onions, chop ginger and garlic, finely and put into the deep pot with 80 ml of cooking oil or two table spoons of ghee, add some Methi and whole zeera. Put on a gas mark four and occasionally stir it till onions turn brownish. Add one tea spoon of salt, half of chilli powder, half of turmeric powder, half of curry powder, half of paprika, two spoons of tomato puree. Heat it for few minutes then add chopped tomatoes with little water into the pot and heat on the gas occasionally stirring till it turns into a paste. Add quarter inch thick and two inches long chopped red pepper, finely chopped spring onions.

Slice the four chicken breasts into two inches long and half inch thick slices. Put them into the pot and fry it in the paste till they go brown, like half cook. Add 25 ml of water, let it simmer for a while to let it thicken up, or the water added is evaporated. At this point the chicken should be cooked (make sure chicken is cooked) Put brandy in the pot, mix well. Cut the fresh coriander finely, and sprinkle over the curry with some gram masala, cover the pot for a minute. Now Chicken Sharabi is ready to serve with rice Nan or Chapatti your choice

54

Chicken Dansak

Three onions (Large)
Half inch of ginger
Six clove garlic
100 Grams plum tomatoes
80 ml cooking oil
Four breast of Chicken (diced)
Fresh coriander (finely chopped)
Two table spoon of tomato puree
125 grams of red lentils

Dice the onion as fine as you can, chop the garlic and ginger put them into a pan with 80 ml of cooking oil. Put on a gas mark 4 add few pinches of Methi and jeera. Fry them for five minutes till onions starts turning brown.

Add one tea spoon of salt, half of chili powder of turmeric powder, one of curry powder, spoon of tomato puree, and 100 grams of plum tomato, stir it well and let it simmer for next 10 minutes, occasionally stirring.

Now add the diced chicken to the pot, mix well and turn the gas down to mark 3. Let it simmer for 10 minutes, occasionally stirring.

Now add 125gms of lentils (ensure they are thoroughly washed) and approximately three quarter liter of boiling water. Let it simmer another 10 to 15 minutes then add freshly chopped coriander and sprinkle some garam masala into the curry.

Chicken Dansak is ready to serve with rice, Nan or chapatti.

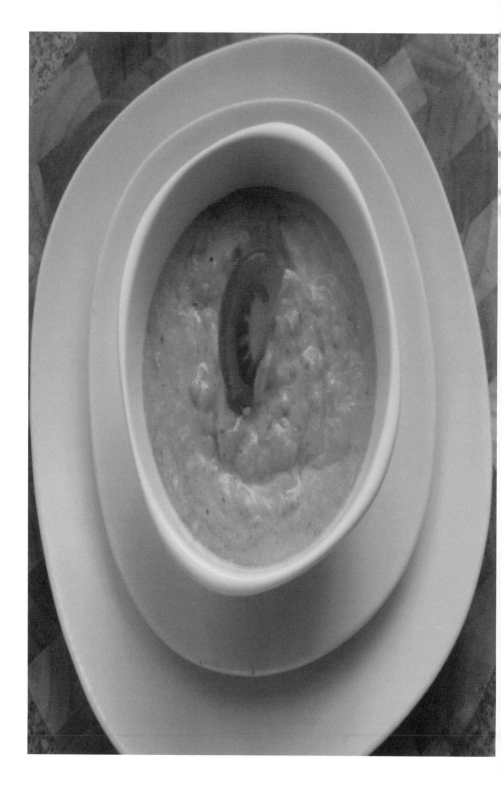

Chicken Kormas

Two chicken Breasts
Two large onions
Quarter inch ginger
Two or Three cloves of garlic
100 grams Coconut cream
Two table spoon of grind coconuts
Half pint of single cream
50 ml of cooking oil or Ghee

Korma is a very mild dish, Chop and dice the onions as fine as you can and put into a pot with finely chopped ginger and garlic, put 50 ml cooking oil or ghee and start cooking on gas mark four. Cook it till the onions go soft and brownish in color. Now add spices, but only this time, because it's a mild curry, we go easy on them. Add half a tea spoon of salt, quarter of chilies powder, half of curry powder, one of turmeric powder. Mix them well and allow it to simmer for few minutes. Now add two table spoons of tomato puree, and keep on heat or ten minutes. Add quarter pint of hot water and liquidize the mixture to a smooth paste.

Cut the chickens into small pieces and put into the pot to cook for fifteen minutes. Now add two table spoons of coconut cream and some single cream to your own taste and how thick you like your Korma. After ten minutes simmering the Korma is ready.

Put in a dish and sprinkle some grinded coconuts on top, the Korma ready to serve with rice, Nan or chapattis.

Chicken Pasanda

Two chicken Breasts
Two large onions
Quarter inch of ginger
Two or Three cloves of garlic
100 grams Coconut cream
Two table spoon of grind coconuts
Half pint of single cream
Small tub of natural yogurt
50 ml of cooking oil or ghee

Pasanda is a very mild dish and to make Pasanda we need to make the curry base, Chop the onions as fine as you can and put into a pot with finely chopped ginger and garlic, add some cooking oil and start cooking on gas mark four . Cook it till the onions go soft and brownish in colour. Now add spices, but only this time, because it's a mild curry, we go easy on them! Add half a tea spoon of salt, quarter of chilies powder, half of curry powder, one of turmeric powder. Mix them well and let it simmer for few minutes. Now add two table spoons of tomato puree, and keep on heat for ten minutes. Add quarter pint of hot water, now liquidize the mixture to a smooth paste.

Cut chickens into small pieces and put into the pot to cook for fifteen minutes. Now add two table spoon of coconut cream and some single cream to your own taste, depending on how thick or thin you like Pasanda. As I said earlier Pasanda is a mild dish, and we add some natural yogurt (according to our liking or taste). Leave it to simmer for five minutes, when it comes to boil Pasanda is ready.

Put in a dish and sprinkle some pistachio and cashew nuts on top.

Chicken Patias

Three large onions
Three clove of garlic
Quarter inch of ginger
Two Serving spoons of Patia sauce
Two table spoon of tomato puree
Four Breast of chickens

Patia is a sweet and sour dish, which is smooth too. To make it we put three large onions finely chopped into a deep pan, along with finely chopped ginger and garlic, add 80 ml of cooking oil and place on gas mark four. Cook it by regularly stirring till the onions go brown. Now time to add spices to the mix, remember it's a mild dish so we have to go easy on them. Put half tea spoon of salt, half of chili powder, one of curry powder, one of turmeric powder, two spoons of tomato puree, mix them well before leaving to simmer for five minutes. Turn down the gas to mark three. As I mentioned earlier it's a very smooth dish, so we have to liquidize the mixture in the pot until it becomes a smooth past.

Cut the chickens into small pieces and put them into the pot, keep stirring and cook till they turn brownish before adding half a pint of water. Let it simmer for ten minutes. Add two spoons of Patia sauce into pot and mix it, let it simmer for five minutes.

Patia is ready to serve to three to four people with rice, chapatti or Nan, it's your choice.

Chicken Chasinies

Three large onions
Two clove of garlic
Quarter inch of ginger
Two Serving spoons of Patia sauce
Two table spoon of tomato puree
Four Breast of chickens
50 ml of cooking oil or Ghee

Chicken Chasini is a sweet and sour but very mild dish that is very smooth as well. To make it we put three large onions finely diced into a deep pan, along with finely chopped ginger and garlic, 50 ml of cooking oil on gas mark four. Cook it by regularly stirring till the onions go brown. Now time to add spices into the mix. Remember it's a mild dish so we go easy on them. Put half tea spoon of salt, half of chili powder, one of curry powder, one of turmeric powder, two spoons of tomato puree, mix them well and let it simmer for five minutes. Turn down the heat to gas - mark three. As I mentioned earlier it's a very smooth dish, so we have to liquidize the mixture in the pot until it becomes a smooth past.

Cut the chickens into small pieces and put them into the pot, keep stirring and cook till they turn brownish before adding half a pint of water. Let it simmer for ten minutes. Add two spoons of Patia sauce into pot and put one third of a pint of single cream mix it, let it simmer for five minutes.

Chicken Chasini is ready to serve to three to four people with rice, chapatti or Nan, it's your choice.

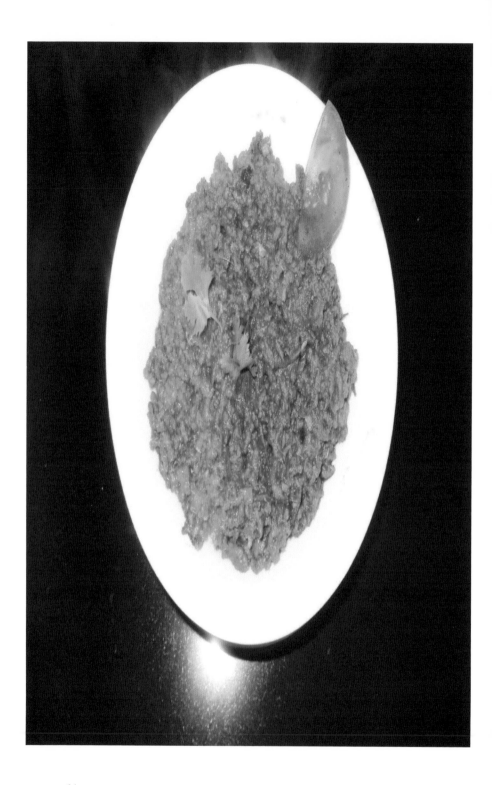

Mince Curry

Three medium size onions
Half an inch of ginger
Six cloves garlic
Three spring onions
Two or three medium size tomatoes
Fresh coriander
500 grams of Lamb or Beef Mince
50 ml of cooking oil

To make a mince curry is like any other curry, we need to make turka. Chop the onions into small pieces, and also chop ginger and garlic very fine with two spoons of Methi, one of Jeera and then put into a deep pot with 50 ml of cooking oil, put on a gas mark four and let it cook for ten fifteen minutes. Add some chopped green chilies if you like it bit hot according to your taste. Waite till onions turns brown. It is now time to add some spices. Add a tea spoon of salt, half of chilies- powder, half of turmeric powder, half of curry powder, half of zeera-powder, half of Dhania- powder. At this stage it will be nice to add some black Lychee and cloves for extra flavor. Add two or three medium size chopped tomatoes, a table spoon of tomato-puree, and mix them all very well and let it simmer on low heat for ten minutes.

Now add the Mince to the curry. You can add green peas or potatoes, whatever you fancy and cook it for forty to forty five minutes, regularly stirring after every ten fifteen minutes.

Add chopped coriander and some Garam-masala, sprinkle over the curry. Mince curry is ready to serve with Nan, Rice Chapatti.

Kofta Curry

Three medium size onions
Half an inch of ginger
Six cloves garlic
Three to Five spring onions
Two or three medium size tomatoes
Fresh coriander
500 grams of Lamb or Beef Mince
Two Eggs
50 ml of cooking oil

Kofta curry is in fact a spicy meatball curry. You make meat-balls from mince and cook them into curry.

To make Kofta curry is like any other curry, we need to make turka. Chop the onions into small pieces and also chop ginger and garlic very fine and then put into a deep pot with 50 ml of cooking oil, also add two spoons of Methi, one of Jeera whole and put on a gas mark four and let it cook for ten fifteen minutes. Add some chopped green chilies if you like it bit hot according to your taste. Waite till onions turns brown. It is now time to add some spices.

Add a tea spoon of salt, half of chilies- powder, half of turmeric powder, half of curry powder, half of zeera-powder, half of Dhania- powder.

At this stage it will be nice to add some black Lychee and cloves for flavor. Add two or three medium size chopped tomatoes. Add table spoon of tomato-puree, mix them all very well and let it simmer on low heat for ten minutes.

While turka is getting cooked, we make Kofta. Put the mince into mixing bowl and add half a spoon of salt, chili to season the mince and add two eggs into the mixing bowl, mix them well with your hand till you can make small balls of them. Heat a pot of a litter of water and put meatballs into it to cook for ten minutes. After ten minutes drain the water out

Now add these Kofta into the pot you are cooking turka in and cook it for twenty to twenty five minutes, regularly stirring at ten minutes interval.

Add chopped coriander and some Garam-masala, sprinkle over the curry. Kofta curry is ready to serve with Nan, Rice or Chapatti

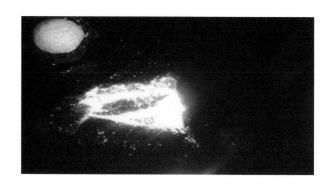

Chapattis

120 grams of chapatti flour
Cold water
Table spoon of cooking oil

To cook chapattis we need dough. To make dough put the chapatti flour in a mixing bowl, add little quantity of cold water into the bowl and start mixing with your fingers. Add more water into it if it is too dry. Keep mixing it until you have dough like consistency which is not too hard or too soft, but good enough to roll with the rolling pin. At this point dough should look like a big round ball of dough. Now add that table spoon of oil on to the sides of bowl. Start mixing the dough against the walls of the bowl till it stops sticking to your hand and mixing bowl. That's dough ready for chapattis.

To make chapatti, as shown in the pictures on left page, first make a round ball of dough of approximately one and a half inch to two inch in size. Then roll that ball on dry chapatti flour. Now on non-sticking surface with a rolling pin, roll that ball into pancake -size round circle. Sprinkle dry chapatti flour on both sides, and start rolling with rolling pin to the size of five or six inch in diameter. That's the raw chapatti ready

Now to cook that raw chapatti we need griddle or in Indian, it's called Tawa. Put the griddle on a gas mark five and let it heat for few minutes before cooking. Put that raw chapatti on hot griddle, and watch, when the top of chapatti turns slightly brown then turn over (watch the griddle is very hot and so is your chapatti). See the picture on opposite page at this stage it looks like a pancake with brown spots. In about 30 seconds later turn it over again. As in picture it looks the same on other side. Keep doing it couple of time until it is cooked as your final chapatti. Enjoy.

Boiled Rice

250grms Rice
120 ml of cooking Oil
Salt

Boiled rice is very easy to cook. Almost everybody knows how to cook it. But to cook nonstick and fluffy rice is bit tricky.

Take a medium size pan, put on gas mark three. Put two pints of boiling water and bring back to boil and add 120ml of oil into it and 250grms basmati rice (You can choose any type of rice only difference would be the boiling time). Boil them for fifteen minutes. Then drain the water, wash the rice with hot water (I emphasize on hot water) thoroughly. And when all water is drained put the rice pot in preheated oven at 200 degree for five minutes. And that is your nice and fluffy boiled rice ready to serve with a leaf of mint or a piece of lemon.

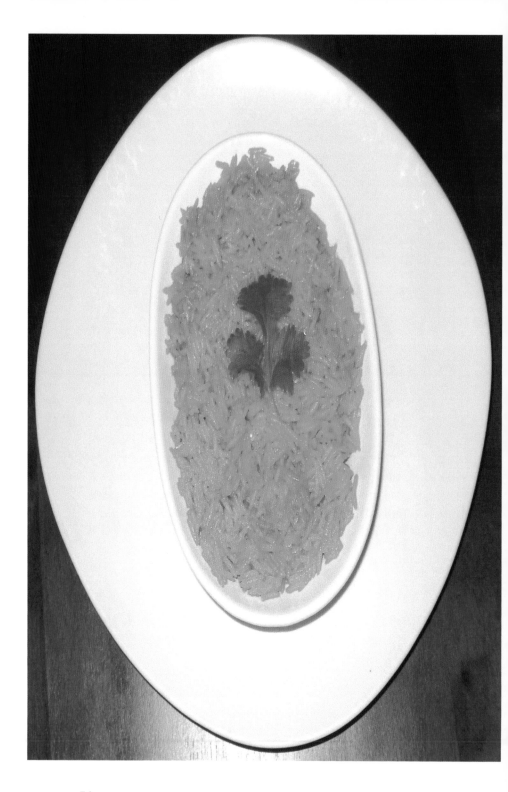

Fried Rice

250grms Basmati Rice
100 ml of Oil
One Small Onion
Tea spoon of Jeera
Two or Three Bay leafs
Tea spoon of salt
One two inch Cinnamon stick

Take a deep pan, put on a gas mark four with 100 ml of oil in it. Add some sliced onions, tea spoon of jeera, two bays leafs, tea spoon of salt and one cinnamon stick, half a dozen cloves and let it fry for five minutes until onions go soft and brownish. Now add a pint of boiling water, with a pinch of egg yellow colour and let it boil. Wash the rice thoroughly with cold water, drain them and put in pot of boiling yellow water. Let it simmer till the water is socked up by the rice. Cover the pot with lid and put in pre-heated oven at 200 degree for five minutes.

Fried rice is ready to serve with a leaf of mint or a piece of lemon on top.

Pilao Rice

250grms Basmati Rice
80 ml of cooking Oil
One Small Onion
Tea spoon of Jeera
Two or Three Bay Leafs
Tea spoon of salt
One two inch Cinnamon sticks
100 grams of Processed Peas

Take a deep pan, put on a gas mark four with oil in it. Put some sliced onions, tea spoon of jeera, two bays leafs a tea spoon of salt and one cinnamon stick and let it fry for five minutes till onions go soft and brownish. Now wash the rice thoroughly with cold water, drain them and put in that pot. Also add a pint of boiling water. Boil it till the water is socked up by the rice. Now add processed green peas and sprinkle some curry powder on the rice to give some colour. Cover the pot with tight lid and put in a pre-heated oven at 200 degrees for five minutes.

After that five minutes take the pot out and with fork separate the rice slowly. With a piece of lemon and sprinkle some coriander Palau is ready to serve.

Biryanies (Chicken)

Two Chicken breasts
80 ml of coocking Oil
Two small Onions
Tea spoon of zeera
Two or three Bay Leafs
One or two inches of Cinnamon stick

Take a deep pan, put on a gas mark four with 80 ml of oil in it. Put some sliced onions, tea spoon of jeera, two bays leafs, tea spoon of salt and one cinnamon stick and let it fry for five minutes till onions go soft and brownish. At this point add half spoon of chilli powder, half spoon of curry powder and half spoon of turmeric powder with a spoon of tomato puree, mix and heat for five minutes. Dice the chickens, wash and put in the pot with green peas, mix and let it simmer on low gas. Keep stirring occasionally till chicken is almost cooked .Wash the rice thoroughly with cold water, drain them and put in that pot with pint of boiling water. Put the gas back to mark four. Boil it till the water is soaked by the rice. Cover the pot with tight lid and put in a pre-heated oven at 200 degrees for five minutes.

After that five minutes take the pot out and with fork separate the rice slowly. With a piece of lemon and sprinkle some coriander Chicken Biryani is ready to serve.

Index

Printed in Great Britain
by Amazon

42869190R00048